S0-BRR-999

Reading Mastery Plus
SRA
Plus

Activities Across the Curriculum

Level 4

Siegfried Engelmann
Susan Hanner

A Division of The McGraw-Hill Companies

Columbus, Ohio

www.sra4kids.com

SRA/McGraw-Hill

A Division of The **McGraw·Hill** *Companies*

Copyright © 2002 by SRA/McGraw-Hill.

All rights reserved. Except as permitted under the United States Copyright Act, no part of this publication may be reproduced or distributed in any form or by any means, or stored in a database or retrieval system, without the prior written permission of the publisher, unless otherwise indicated.

Send all inquiries to:
SRA/McGraw-Hill
8787 Orion Place
Columbus, OH 43240-4027

Printed in the United States of America.

ISBN 0-07-569149-3

4 5 6 7 8 9 MAL 06 05

Introduction

What Is the Program?

Activities Across the Curriculum, Level 4 contains activities that can be used to extend and reinforce the skills your students are acquiring as they progress through *Reading Mastery Plus, Level 4.* The activities cover a range of content areas, including science, social studies, and geography.

How Does the Program Work?

The program provides 33 activities, most of which have blackline master student material. Each activity is correlated to a specific lesson range in *Reading Mastery Plus, Level 4.*

The activity expands on the skills or information presented in those specified lessons. The lesson number references appear on each page of the teacher directions. In addition, each activity specifies the content area being explored and states the objective.

To use the program:
- Select the activities that you wish to present and schedule them at a time when the students have completed the targeted lessons in *Reading Mastery Plus, Level 4.*

- Schedule sufficient time for the activity, but don't allow so much time that activity work seriously impedes students' progress through *Reading Mastery Plus, Level 4.*

- If a blackline master is involved, provide students with copies of the student material.

- Give students feedback as they work on the activity and praise individuals or small groups that work well.

- Check students' work by referring to the answers listed under Evaluation/ Answers in the teacher directions.

Success with Activities Across the Curriculum

Activities Across the Curriculum, Level 4 will give your students further practice in using their reading skills. By gaining proficiency in reading and writing tasks that span the curriculum, they will be more prepared to apply their skills to the challenges of everyday living.

Table of Contents

ACTIVITY 1

Lessons 14–16

Science: Analyzing Features/Comparing Creatures

Materials: Blackline Master 1, writing materials

Objective: Students will analyze features of some animals in Alaska.

Directions: Ask students to read the directions and the information on Blackline Master 1. Then have students work in groups of three or four to complete the feature analysis.

On a separate sheet of paper, have students write a paragraph comparing two of the animals.

Evaluation/Answers: Students' feature analyses should reflect an awareness of some of the differences between and among at least four animals of the region. Paragraphs should pinpoint similarities between two animals as well as unique features of each.

ACTIVITY 2

Lesson 21

Science: Tracking the Weather

Materials: Blackline Master 2, writing materials

Objective: Students will observe, record, and summarize weather conditions in their area for one week.

Directions: Ask students to read the directions and the information on Blackline Master 2. Then have students work in pairs to complete the daily weather chart for one week. If students do not have a thermometer to measure the temperature outside, provide that information for them.

Have students write on a separate sheet of paper a paragraph that summarizes the weather this week—number of clear days, range of temperatures, and so on.

Evaluation/Answers: Chart information should be based on accurate, verifiable data.

ACTIVITY 3

Lessons 23–24

Science: Dinosaurs

Materials: Blackline Master 3, writing materials

Objective: Students will write two to four paragraphs comparing and contrasting two dinosaurs.

Directions: Have students read the directions and information on Blackline Master 3. Ask them to note similarities and differences between the two dinosaurs. Students should write two comparison paragraphs about the dinosaurs.

Evaluation/Answers: The first paragraph should relate how the two dinosaurs were alike; the second, how they were different.

ACTIVITY 4

Lessons 24–32

Writing: Using a Story Map

Materials: Blackline Master 4, writing materials, textbook A

Objective: Students will use a story map to summarize a story.

Directions: Ask students to read the directions and information on Blackline Master 4.

Evaluation/Answers: Students' stories should follow the organization of their story maps. Stories should have a clear beginning, middle, and end.

ACTIVITY 5

Lesson 33

Science: Volcanoes

Materials: Writing materials

Objective: Students will write a news article about a volcano eruption.

Directions: Draw on the board.

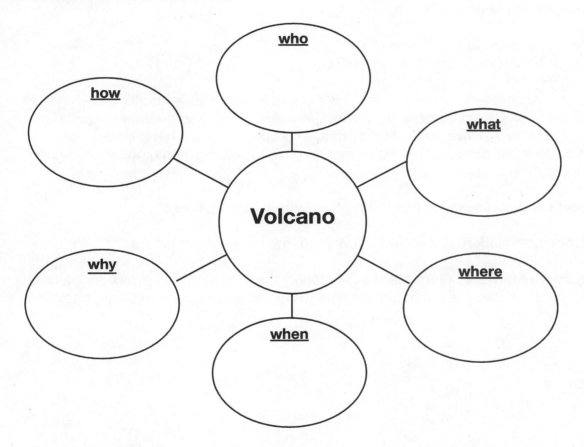

Have students imagine they are near the scene of a volcano eruption. Refer to the diagram as students discuss what happens during a volcano eruption. Ask questions like "What did you see? Smell? Hear? Feel?" and "Where did it happen? When?"

Write students' responses in the circles. Add circles as needed.

Ask students to write a news article telling what happened and what it was like. Remind students to use the diagram when writing their news articles. Articles should be several paragraphs long. Have students read their articles to the class.

Evaluation/Answers: Students' articles should include sensory images of a volcano, as well as important facts relating to *who, what, where, when, why,* and *how.*

ACTIVITY 6

Lesson 36

Science: Inventors

Materials: Letter-writing materials

Objective: Students will write letters to real or imaginary inventors explaining how their inventions are currently used.

Directions: Write on the board:

What I like about your invention.
What I don't like about your invention.

Have students select a product they use frequently (machines, appliances, tools, or their everyday school utensils like pencils, erasers, pens, and so on). Students are to write a letter to the inventor of that particular product telling what they like and dislike about the product. The letter should have two paragraphs, one for likes and one for dislikes.

Students should use good business letter form in these letters.

• Upon completion, call on individual students to read their letters.

Evaluation/Answers: Students should identify the invention and provide a general explanation of how it is used. Letters should be written in the appropriate business letter form.

ACTIVITY 7

Lessons 41–43
Science: Designing an Invention

Materials: Drawing materials, writing materials

Objective: Students will draw a diagram of an invention they would like to create, and they will write a brief explanation of why the invention is needed, what it does, and how it works.

Directions: Have students work in small groups to describe an invention. Encourage them to think of a problem they encounter in their day-to-day lives and think of a possible device to help solve the problem.

Students should give their invention a name and write a short explanation of why it is needed, what it would do, and how it would work. Students should draw a detailed diagram of the invention, labeling its parts and explaining how the parts work.

Drawings and explanations can be mounted on large construction paper and posted for the class to share.

Evaluation/Answers: Students' drawings and explanations should reflect an awareness of a problem to solve. Explanations should be clear. Drawings should be reasonable.

ACTIVITY 8

Lessons 45–46
Science: An Electric Circuit

Materials: Blackline Master 5, writing materials

Objective: Students will study a diagram showing how a simple electric circuit works and write brief explanations about it.

Directions: Have students read the directions and the information on Blackline Master 5. Then have students answer the questions about how an electric circuit works.

Evaluation/Answers: Students' explanations may be brief but should reflect an understanding of the diagram.

ACTIVITY 9

Lessons 48–51

Writing: Creating an Advertisement

Materials: Writing materials; optional: magazines

Objective: Students will create an advertisement for an invention they want to sell.

Directions: Have students create an advertisement to sell the invention created in Activity 7.

What problems does this invention solve? To help students get started, ask them to write down a list of benefits to the users if they buy and use this invention. Encourage students to create an ad that uses an illustration as well as text. You may want to have several magazines on hand for students to look at to get ideas.

Ads should be presented to the class.

Evaluation/Answers: Students' advertisements should state or visually demonstrate one or more benefits to the user.

ACTIVITY 10

Lesson 53

Math and Science: The Solar System

Materials: Blackline Master 6, calculator

Objective: Students will use math and information provided in a chart about the solar system to solve math problems and to write a math story problem of their own.

Directions: Have students read the directions and the information on Blackline Master 6. Then have students answer the questions that follow.

Evaluation/Answers:

1. 365.26 times number of years in age
2. number of days old divided by 687
3. number of days old divided by 225
4. 3,703
5. Answers will vary but should require math computation and use information from the chart.

ACTIVITY 11

Lesson 56
Social Studies: Time Lines

Materials: Blackline Master 7, textbook A

Objective: After reading the story on pages 280–281 of textbook A, students will put the events in the correct sequence, then complete a time line of those events.

Directions: Have students read the directions and the information on Blackline Master 7. Then have students number the events in the sequence they occurred.

After students have numbered the events in order, they should complete the time line.

Evaluation/Answers:

Correct sequence of events:
1. Wendy leaves Canada by jet.
2. Wendy lands in Tokyo.
3. Reporters meet the travelers at the airport.
4. Wendy and others take a bus to the space station.
5. Wendy talks to Bob.
6. Sidney shouts, "I'm here!"
7. Wendy gets out her pass and medical report.
8. The travelers prepare to board *Traveler Four*.

Students should write the events in the correct sequence with the first event at the bottom and the last event at the top.

ACTIVITY 12

Lessons 61–62
Science: Facts About Jupiter

Materials: Writing materials

Objective: Students will write and act out an interview with a famous scientist.

Directions: The reporter is to interview the scientist to find out about Jupiter and its moons. Students first prepare a list of questions to ask a scientist who has just returned from two weeks on one of Jupiter's moons. Then have students break into pairs. Have them imagine that one of them is a famous scientist and the other is a famous television news reporter. Students should write their interview questions and responses. Then have students act out the dialogue between the scientist and the reporter.

Evaluation/Answers: Students' interviews should reflect a basic knowledge of the planet Jupiter. The interviews should also use dialogue correctly.

ACTIVITY 13

Lessons 64–66
Music: Songs That Tell a Story

Materials: Writing materials

Objective: Students will retell the story about Wendy and Sidney in the form of a song or poem.

Directions: Ask students to select a melody or tune that they like and know well. Have students work in groups to write the song of Wendy and Sidney and their trip to Io. The song should have lines that rhyme. For example, a student could write a story-poem that could be sung to the tune of "Yankee Doodle" or "This Land Is My Land."

Ask for volunteers (or groups) to sing their songs to the class.

Evaluation/Answers: Students' songs should incorporate key events of the story, using rhyme if possible or appropriate.

Lesson 69

Language: Giving a Speech to Persuade

Materials: Writing materials

Objective: Students will prepare and present a persuasive speech.

Directions: Have students imagine that they want to get an after-school job grooming dogs.

Write on the board: Main goal—to get a job at Dog Wash

> Reason 1: I like dogs a lot.
> Reason 2: Dogs like me.
> Reason 3: I am a hard worker.
> Reason 4: I have experience washing dogs.

Suggest that students pretend these are the reasons they should be hired. Have students write their speeches, filling in details.

Have students take turns presenting their arguments to the class. One student can play the role of owner while another student applies for the job.

Evaluation/Answers: Students' speeches should contain clearly stated reasons that support their goal or opinion. The reasons should be presented in a logical order.

ACTIVITY 15

Lesson 74

Math: Selling Tickets

Materials: Writing materials

Objective: Students will compute how much money would be made if 80 tickets to an animal show sold for $1 each; and if $100 needed to be made, how many more people would need to buy tickets at the old rate of $1 or a new rate of $2.

Directions: Tell students they have been put in charge of ticket sales for the annual animal show. Here are some problems to solve:

1. Last year, tickets were sold for $1 each, and 80 people attended the show. Ask students to compute how much money was made last year (1 x 80 = $80).

2. Tell students that this year it will cost more to put on the show. Ask them how much they should charge if they need to make $90, and only 30 people attend (90 ÷ 30 = $3).

3. Finally, ask students how much money they would make if 100 tickets sold for $2 each (2 x 100 = $200).

Evaluation/Answers:

1. Money made last year: $80

2. They should charge $3.00 per ticket if they want to make $90 and know that they will sell only 30 tickets.

3. They would make $200.

ACTIVITY 16

Lesson 82

Geography: Locating Points on a Map

Materials: Blackline Master 8

Objective: Students will locate points on a map.

Directions: Tell students to read the information and directions on Blackline Master 8. Then have students answer the questions about the map.

Evaluation/Answers:

1. Denver
2. Boise
3. Rocky Mountains
4. Utah
5. Colorado River

Lesson 86

Math: Calculating Water Pressure

Materials: Writing materials

Objective: Students will be able to compute water pressure at different depths.

Directions: Explain to students that water pressure on the body increases as a person goes deeper under water. Divers must be careful at great depths because the pressure can have dangerous, and even fatal, effects.

Write the following information on the board:

> If the water pressure at 33 feet below the surface of the water is twice as great as the pressure at the surface, how much greater is the water pressure at 66 feet? At 99 feet?

Ask students to continue the pattern up to about 200 feet.

Evaluation/Answers:

At 33 feet, the pressure is 2 times what it is at the surface.
At 66 feet, the pressure is 3 times what it is at the surface.
At 99 feet, the pressure is 4 times what it is at the surface.
At 132 feet, the pressure is 5 times what it is at the surface.
At 165 feet, the pressure is 6 times what it is at the surface.
At 198 feet, the pressure is 7 times what it is at the surface.

ACTIVITY 18

Lesson 87

Geography: Getting Information from Maps

Materials: Blackline Master 9

Objective: Students use a map to identify states that border the ocean, use a map scale to figure distance between two points on a map, and use direction to locate places on a map.

Directions: Have students read the directions and study the map on Blackline Master 9. Then ask them to work independently to follow the directions and answer the questions.

Evaluation/Answers:

1. Virginia, North Carolina, South Carolina, Georgia, Florida (VA, NC, SC, GA, FL)
2. approximately 1,200 miles
3. Gulf of Mexico
4. Answers will vary depending on student-generated questions. Students' questions should reflect an understanding of the information on the map.

ACTIVITY 19

Lesson 88

Health: Dealing with Emergencies

Materials: Blackline Master 10; writing materials; materials for making posters; optional: magazines

Objective: Students will create a poster explaining how to deal with a specific kind of emergency.

Directions: Have students read the directions and information on Blackline Master 10. Then assign them to groups of 3 or 4 to complete the activity.

Evaluation/Answers: Students' posters should list specific steps for preventing and handling an emergency situation.

ACTIVITY 20

Lesson 89
Writing: Using Dialogue

Materials: Blackline Master 11, writing materials

Objective: Students will use dialogue in a written narrative about characters who are in a dangerous situation.

Directions: Have students read the directions and information on Blackline Master 11. Then ask them to work independently to complete the activity.

Evaluation/Answers: Students' dialogues should address the problem. Students should indent for every new speaker, and they should use quotation marks correctly to enclose direct quotes.

ACTIVITY 21

Lessons 94–97
Language: Using Adverbs

Materials: Blackline Master 12, writing materials

Objective: Students will understand the use of adverbs in sentences.

Directions: Have students read the directions and information on Blackline Master 12. Then ask them to work independently to complete the activity.

Evaluation/Answers: Students' sentences will vary but should use adverbs correctly.

ACTIVITY 22

Lesson 105

Science: What's the Matter?

Materials: Blackline Master 13

Objective: Students will categorize examples of matter in solid, liquid, and gas form.

Directions: Have students read the directions and information on Blackline Master 13.

Evaluation/Answers:

1. solid
2. liquid
3. solid
4. gas
5. liquid
6. gas
7. solid
8. solid
9. liquid
10. solid

ACTIVITY 23

Lesson 117

Science: Comparing Animals' Sizes

Materials: Blackline Master 14

Objective: Students will use information provided in a bar graph to answer questions about relative sizes of sea animals.

Directions: Have students read the directions and information on Blackline Master 14. Then direct them to work independently to complete the activity.

Evaluation/Answers:

1. 10 meters
2. blue whale, 28 meters long
3. 9 meters
4. 4 meters (stingray)
5. sperm whale

ACTIVITY 24

Lessons 119–121

Art: Drawing Muscles and Bones

Materials: Drawing materials, textbook B; optional: reference books

Objective: Students will draw a diagram of the muscles and bones in the human arm.

Directions: Have students refer to their textbooks or to reference books, if available. Ask them about how the muscles in a human arm work. Discuss how muscles work.

Students work in pairs to draw color diagrams of the muscles in a human arm. Students label the biceps and triceps.

Evaluation/Answers: Students' drawings should show a basic representation of the arm bones, with biceps and triceps muscles labeled.

ACTIVITY 25

Lessons 122–123

Writing and Science: Explaining How the Circulatory System Works

Materials: Blackline Master 15

Objective: Students will write a paragraph explaining how blood circulates through the human body, using a diagram to help explain the system.

Directions: Have students read the directions and information on Blackline Master 15. Then have them work in pairs to complete the activity.

Evaluation/Answers: Students' explanations should reflect the information provided in Lessons 122 and 123. Diagrams should be properly labeled (heart, lungs, blood vessels).

ACTIVITY 26

Lesson 123

Health: Taking Your Pulse

Materials: Blackline Master 16, clock or watch

Objective: Students will chart their pulses while sitting quietly, then after jumping up and down.

Directions: Have students read the directions and information on Blackline Master 16. Then ask them to work independently to complete the activity. Assist them in timing the one-minute segments.

Evaluation/Answers: Students' results will vary. Students should conclude that increased physical exertion causes the heart rate to speed up.

ACTIVITY 27

Lessons 124–125

Science and Art: Drawing Your Nervous System

Materials: Blackline Master 17, large pieces of drawing paper (or newspaper taped together)

Objective: Students will understand the structure of the nervous system.

Directions: Have students read the directions and information on Blackline Master 17. Then ask them to work in pairs to complete the activity. (Students can draw their outlines on pieces of drawing paper or newspaper taped together.)

Evaluation/Answers: Students' outlines will vary, but their reproductions of the nervous system should be accurate copies of the model supplied.

ACTIVITY 28

Lessons 126–127
Writing Poetry: Using the Senses in Writing

Materials: Blackline Master 18

Objective: Students will write a poem using sensory language.

Directions: Have students read the directions and information on Blackline Master 18, then complete the activity.

Evaluation/Answers: Students' poems will vary but should incorporate language that appeals to the senses.

ACTIVITY 29

Lesson 129
Health: Steps to a Healthy Body

Materials: Blackline Master 19, poster-making materials

Objective: Students will create a poster that lists ways to stay healthy.

Directions: Students should read the directions and information on Blackline Master 19, then make their notes and complete the activity.

Evaluation/Answers: Students' posters should address the importance of good eating habits, exercise, and sleep.

ACTIVITY 30

Lesson 132
Geography: Reading a Weather Map

Materials: Blackline Master 20

Objective: Students will read and use a weather map.

Directions: Have students read the directions and information on Blackline Master 20. Then have them answer the questions.

Evaluation/Answers:

1. Chicago, Detroit
2. snow, cloudy, 26/12
3. Stevens Point, Duluth, Bismarck, Winnipeg
4. St. Louis

ACTIVITY 31

Lesson 133
Social Studies: Comparing the Poles

Materials: Blackline Master 21

Objective: Students will compare the North Pole and the South Pole.

Directions: Have students read the directions and information on Blackline Master 21. Then have them complete the activity.

Evaluation/Answers: Students' passages should incorporate information about what is the same and what is different.

Lesson 134

Language: Compound Words

Materials: Blackline Master 22

Objective: Students will create a list of compound words.

Directions: Have students read the directions and information on Blackline Master 22. Then have them answer the questions.

Evaluation/Answers:

1. birthday
2. doorbell
3. snowflakes
4. schoolwork
5. earthquake
6. bathtub
7. daylight
8. anywhere
9. sidewalk
10. Answers will vary.

ACTIVITY 33

Lesson 139

Art: Making a Book Jacket

Materials: Paper for making book jacket (for example, construction paper, gift wrap, brown paper bags, notebook paper)

Objective: Students will design a book jacket for a book they would like to read or write.

Directions: Ask students to think of a book they would like to write or a subject they would like to read about. Have them invent a title for this book. Then ask students to create a book jacket for the book.

Each book jacket front should clearly state the title and author (the student). Students should draw a picture or graphic design to go on the front as well. On the back, students should write a short summary of what the book is about and why a person would want to read it. The summary should "sell" the reader on the book.

Students could use construction paper or two sheets of notebook paper for their book jackets.

Evaluation/Answers: Students' book jackets should reflect an awareness of the structure and design of book coverings; creative approaches should be encouraged.

Blackline Masters

ACTIVITY 1: Analyzing Features/ Comparing Creatures

Directions: You're going to complete the table below to tell about the features of Alaskan animals. In the first column, list at least four animals that live in Alaska. Then fill in the boxes to tell about the animals' features. Write **Y** for **yes** and **N** for **no** to tell whether the animal has that feature. The chart has been started for you. Add animals and features to the chart.

Write a paragraph on a separate sheet of paper. Compare two of the animals that you listed on your chart. Tell how they are the same. Then tell 2 ways they are different from each other.

FEATURE

ANIMAL	Warm-Blooded (like humans)	Cold-Blooded (like fish)	Hunt in Packs	Eat Plants
Killer Whale				

© SRA/McGraw-Hill. Permission is granted to reproduce this page for classroom use.

ACTIVITY 2: Tracking the Weather

Directions: Observe and note the weather changes in your area for one week. Use the chart below to track the weather.

At the end of the week, write a paragraph summarizing the weather changes that took place during the week.

Day	Date	High Temperature	Low Temperature	Cloud Cover	Wind Direction	Rain or Snow
1						
2						
3						
4						
5						
6						
7						

© SRA/McGraw-Hill. Permission is granted to reproduce this page for classroom use.

Blackline Master 2

ACTIVITY 3: Dinosaurs

Directions: Study the chart below. It lists some features of two different dinosaurs. Note how the dinosaurs were alike and how they were different. Then write two paragraphs on lined paper. In the first paragraph tell how they were alike. In the second paragraph tell how they were different.

Tyrannosaurus Rex	Brontosaurus
was a dinosaur	was a dinosaur
lived about 70 million years ago	lived about 150 million years ago
meat-eating reptile	plant-eating reptile
walked upright on two hind legs	walked on four legs
about 20 feet tall, 47 feet long	about 15 feet tall, 70 feet long
lived mostly on land	lived mostly in water
had a short neck, large head	had a long neck, small head
had a long tail	had a long tail
was a fierce killer	was harmless
is now extinct	is now extinct

© SRA/McGraw-Hill. Permission is granted to reproduce this page for classroom use.

ACTIVITY 4: Using a Story Map

Directions: Use the story map below to tell the main things that happened in the story of Oomoo and Oolak. Be sure to keep the events in order, and make sure your story has a beginning, a middle and an end.

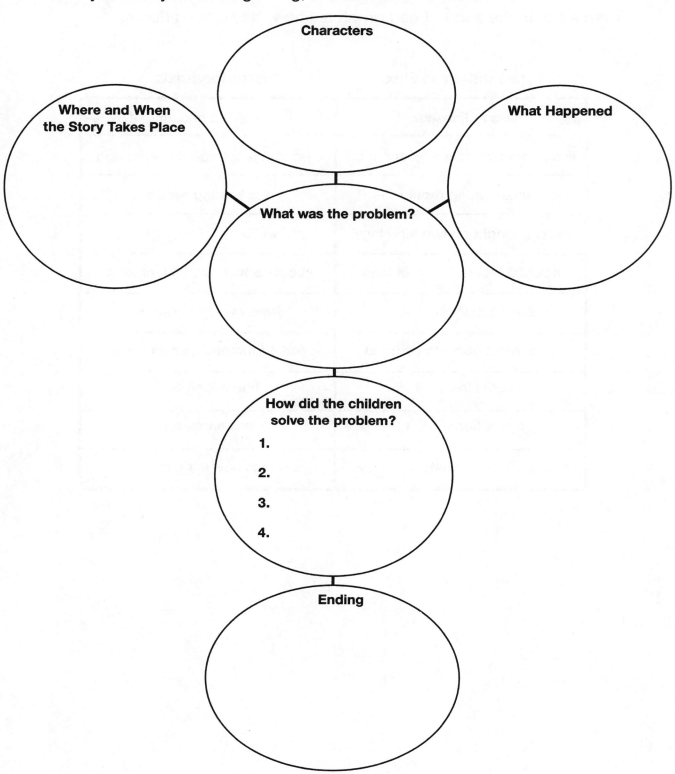

© SRA/McGraw-Hill. Permission is granted to reproduce this page for classroom use.

ACTIVITY 8: An Electric Circuit

Directions: Look at the diagrams and explanations below. Then write a short explanation to answer each question.

Simple Electric Circuit

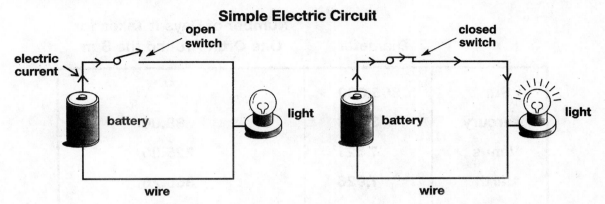

The electric power is in the battery. The electric current moves from the battery, through the wire, to the switch.

If the switch is closed, the charges can go through the switch. The light will go on.

If the switch is **open,** the electricity cannot move through the switch, so the light will not go on.

1. What happens when the switch is open?

_____

_____

2. What happens when the switch is closed?

_____

_____

3. What happens if the battery has no power in it?

_____

_____

4. What happens if the light bulb is burned out?

_____

_____

© SRA/McGraw-Hill. Permission is granted to reproduce this page for classroom use.

ACTIVITY 10:   The Solar System

Directions: Study the information provided in the chart. Then answer the questions.

	Diameter	Number of Days It Takes for One Orbit Around the Sun
Sun	865,000	–
Mercury	3,031	88.00
Venus	7,521	225.00
Earth	7,926	365.26
Mars	4,223	687.00
Jupiter	88,846	4,333.00
Saturn	74,898	10,759.00
Uranus	31,763	30,685.00
Neptune	30,775	60,190.00
Pluto	1,430	90,800.00

1. How many days old are you on Earth? _____

2. If you lived on Mars, one year would be 687 days.

   How many years old would you be? _____

3. How many years old would you be on Venus? _____

4. The diameter of Earth is larger than the diameter of Mars. How much

   larger? _____

5. Use the information in the chart to make up a story problem of your own. Provide the answers, too.

   _____

   _____

© SRA/McGraw-Hill. Permission is granted to reproduce this page for classroom use.

Blackline Master 6

ACTIVITY 11:   Time Lines

Directions: Read the story for lesson 56, "A Surprise at the Space Station," on pages 280–281. Then number the following events to show which was first, which was next and so forth.

____ Reporters meet the travelers at the airport.

____ Sidney shouts, "I'm here!"

____ Wendy talks to Bob.

____ Wendy gets out her pass and medical report.

____ Wendy lands in Tokyo.

____ Wendy leaves Canada by jet.

____ The travelers prepare to board *Traveler Four*.

____ Wendy and others take a bus to the space station.

Use the time line to show the order of events. At the bottom, write the first event. At the top, write the last event. Arrange the other events where they belong.

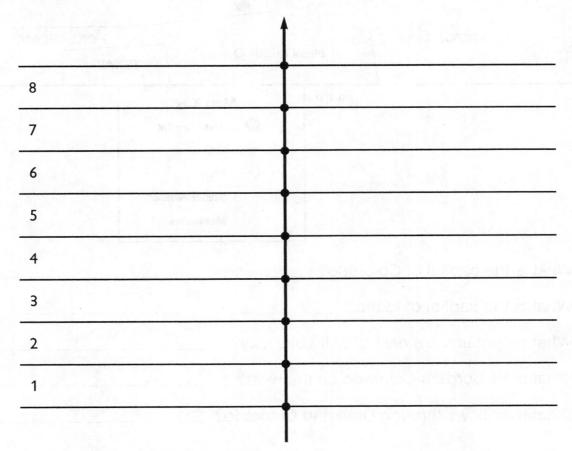

© SRA/McGraw-Hill. Permission is granted to reproduce this page for classroom use.

ACTIVITY 16:   Locating Points on a Map

Directions: Study the map below. Then follow the directions and answer the questions using the map key to help you.

1. What is the capital of Colorado? _____

2. What is the capital of Idaho? _____

3. What mountains are east of Salt Lake City? _____

4. What state borders Colorado on the west? _____

5. What river flows through Utah and Colorado? _____

© SRA/McGraw-Hill. Permission is granted to reproduce this page for classroom use.

ACTIVITY 18:   Getting Information from Maps

Directions: Study the map below. Then work on your own to follow the directions and answer the questions.

1. List all the states south of Maryland (MD) that border the Atlantic Ocean.

_____

_____

2. About how far is it from the southern tip of Florida to the Bermuda Islands?

_____

3. What's the name of the body of water that is west of Florida?

_____

_____

4. Write a question that refers to the map. Ask a classmate to answer it.

_____

_____

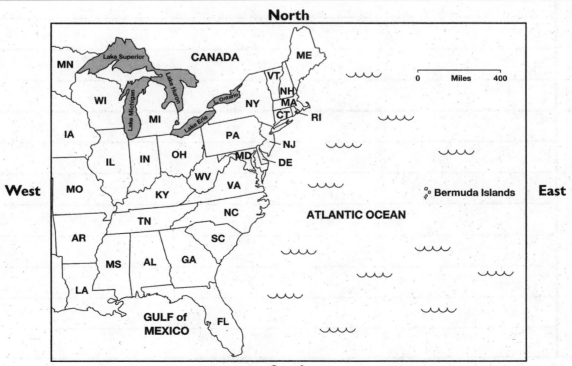

© SRA/McGraw-Hill. Permission is granted to reproduce this page for classroom use.

ACTIVITY 19: Dealing with Emergencies

Directions: Work in a group to make a poster.

Discuss one of the emergency situations listed below. First talk about how to **prevent** such an emergency; then talk about what to do if it happens. Make a list of these things. Use the chart below to help you write down notes for a poster. Then create a poster telling how to handle the emergency. Use a separate sheet of paper or posterboard to make your poster. Include drawings or photographs from magazines.

fire	medical emergency
tornado/hurricane	flood/landslide
accident in the home	drowning

Kind of Emergency

How to Prevent It	
What to Do If It Happens	

© SRA/McGraw-Hill. Permission is granted to reproduce this page for classroom use.

ACTIVITY 20: Using Dialogue

Directions: What characters say to each other is called *dialogue.* Here are some examples of dialogue. Each time another speaker begins to speak, start a new paragraph.

Mavis said, "Here's that cave I told you about."

Ken asked, "Do you think it's safe to go in there?"

"Oh, it's no big deal," Mavis said. "What could possibly happen?"

The two of them entered the cave slowly. "Ooooo, eeeeeyaaaaa," howled a voice from the cave.

"Yikes," said Ken. "Let's get out of here. I don't like the sound of this."

Write a dialogue about Ted and Tina. These students are trying to get out of a forest. A fire is moving toward them. Write your dialogue on a separate sheet of paper.

© SRA/McGraw-Hill. Permission is granted to reproduce this page for classroom use.

ACTIVITY 21:   Using Adverbs

Directions: The words below are adverbs. Use each word in a sentence. Write your sentences below. If you need more room, write on the back of this paper.

gently	often	sometimes	tomorrow
especially	actually	immediately	nowhere

1. _____

_____

2. _____

_____

3. _____

_____

4. _____

_____

5. _____

_____

6. _____

_____

7. _____

_____

8. _____

_____

© SRA/McGraw-Hill. Permission is granted to reproduce this page for classroom use.

ACTIVITY 22:   What's the Matter?

Directions: Everything in the world is made of matter. Matter is in one of three forms: **solid, liquid** or **gas**. Ice is a solid. Water is a liquid. Steam is a gas.

Write *solid, liquid* or *gas* to describe each example of matter.

1. hamburger _____

2. cooking oil _____

3. scissors _____

4. air _____

5. milk _____

6. smoke _____

7. rock _____

8. paper _____

9. hot butter _____

10. cold butter _____

© SRA/McGraw-Hill. Permission is granted to reproduce this page for classroom use.

ACTIVITY 23:   Comparing Animals' Sizes

Directions: The bar graph shows the length of some large animals that live in the ocean. Use the graph to answer the questions.

Length of Ocean Animals
(number of meters long)

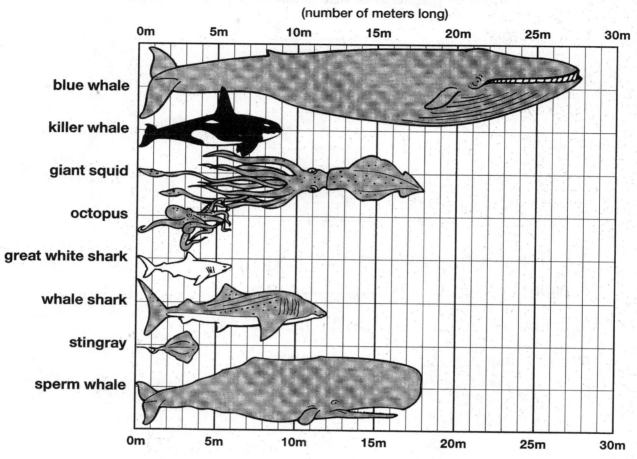

1. How much larger than a giant squid is the blue whale?

   _____ meters.

2. Which is the longest animal shown on the graph? _____

   How long is it? _____ meters.

3. How much smaller than the sperm whale is the killer whale?

   _____ meters.

4. What is the length of the smallest animal shown on the graph?

   _____ meters.

5. Which is larger, the whale shark or the sperm whale? _____

© SRA/McGraw-Hill. Permission is granted to reproduce this page for classroom use.

ACTIVITY 25: Explaining How the Circulatory System Works

Directions: Look at the diagram of the human body. Write a brief explanation of how the circulatory system works. Use these questions to help you.

What color is blood as it leaves the lungs and goes to the heart?

What does the heart do?

Why is the heart called a pump?

What color is blood after it has delivered oxygen to all parts of the body?

The blood that leaves the body parts goes three places.

Where does the blood go first?

Where does it go next?

Where does it go last?

Vena cava

Aorta

Heart

Lungs

Capillaries

_____

_____

_____

_____

_____

_____

_____

© SRA/McGraw-Hill. Permission is granted to reproduce this page for classroom use.

ACTIVITY 26:   Taking Your Pulse

Directions: Put the fingers of your right hand on the inside of your left wrist. You should be able to feel an artery (blood vessel) pound each time your heart beats.

Sit quietly. Then count your heartbeats for one minute.
Write your pulse rate on the chart below.

Now jump up and down 20 times. Take your pulse for one minute.
Write your pulse rate on the chart below.

Compare the two pulse rates. On the lines below the chart, tell how the pulse rates are different. Then tell why they are different.

Pulse Rate Chart

Pulse After Sitting	Pulse After Exercise

_____

_____

_____

_____

_____

_____

_____

_____

© SRA/McGraw-Hill. Permission is granted to reproduce this page for classroom use.

ACTIVITY 27: Drawing Your Nervous System

Directions: With the help of a partner, draw an outline of your body on a large piece of paper or newspaper. Then use the diagram below to help you draw a model of your own nervous system.

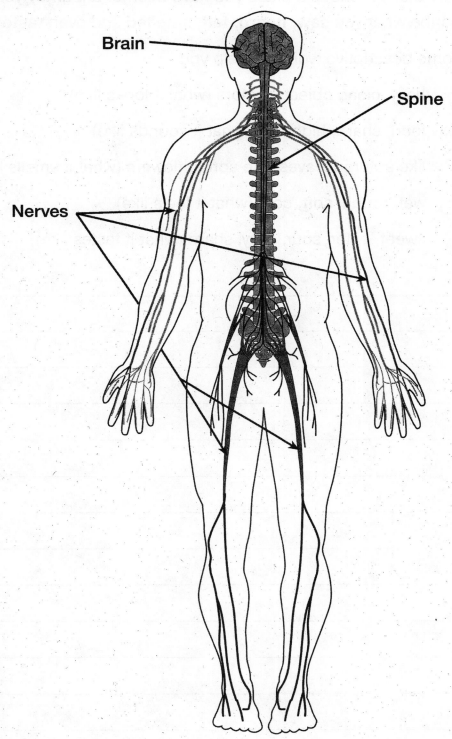

Brain

Spine

Nerves

© SRA/McGraw-Hill. Permission is granted to reproduce this page for classroom use.

ACTIVITY 28: Using the Senses in Writing

Directions: You have learned about how some of your senses work—your senses of touch, smell and taste; your sense of sight; and your sense of hearing. You use your senses to learn about the world around you.

Write a poem that describes a place you have been or a journey you have taken. Describe what you **saw, heard, felt, smelled** and even **tasted.**

Here are some descriptive words to help you:

Sight: hazy, clear, objects, colors (what it looks like)

Hearing: loud, sharp, high, low (what it sounds like)

Smell: like autumn leaves, like spring flowers (what it smells like)

Feeling: wet, rough, soft, cold (what it feels like)

Taste: sweet, bitter, sour, salty, sharp (what it tastes like)

_____

_____

_____

_____

_____

_____

_____

_____

_____

_____

© SRA/McGraw-Hill. Permission is granted to reproduce this page for classroom use.

ACTIVITY 29:   Steps to a Healthy Body

Directions: It is important to take care of your body. What are some ways to keep your body healthy?

Write six ways to keep your body healthy. Then use your list to make a poster called "Steps to a Healthy Body." Use a separate sheet of paper or posterboard for your poster.

Ways to Keep Your Body Healthy

1. _____

_____

2. _____

_____

3. _____

_____

4. _____

_____

5. _____

_____

6. _____

_____

© SRA/McGraw-Hill. Permission is granted to reproduce this page for classroom use.

ACTIVITY 30:   Reading a Weather Map

Directions: Below is a sample of a weather map. It shows some weather conditions that are expected in various areas tomorrow. Maps like these appear in many daily newspapers.

Study the map. Then answer the questions.

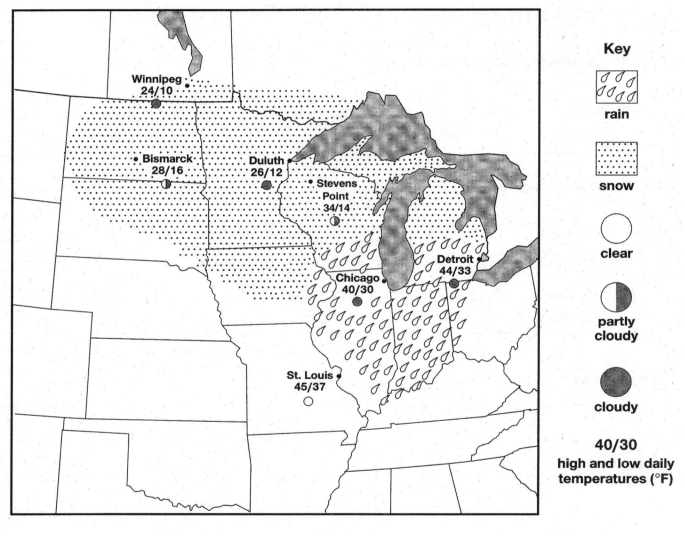

Key

rain

snow

clear

partly cloudy

cloudy

40/30
high and low daily temperatures (°F)

1. Which two cities can expect rain? _____

2. What will the weather be like in Duluth? Show the high and low

   temperatures. _____

3. Name the four cities that will be getting snow. _____

   _____

4. In what city would you expect clear skies? _____

© SRA/McGraw-Hill. Permission is granted to reproduce this page for classroom use.

ACTIVITY 31:   Comparing the Poles

Directions: Think of all the things you now know about the North Pole and the South Pole. List things that are the same about the poles and things that are different about the poles.

After you have finished your list, write a passage that compares the North and South Poles. Write one paragraph about things that are the same. Write another paragraph about things that are different.

What's the same?

_____

_____

_____

_____

_____

What's different?

_____

_____

_____

_____

_____

© SRA/McGraw-Hill. Permission is granted to reproduce this page for classroom use.

ACTIVITY 32:   Compound Words

Directions: A compound word is a word that is made by combining two other words. Combine the words below to make words you know.

birth	quake
door	tub
snow	walk
school	work
earth	bell
bath	where
day	flakes
any	day
side	light

1. _____

2. _____

3. _____

4. _____

5. _____

6. _____

7. _____

8. _____

9. _____

10. Think of another compound word you know. Write it here.

_____

© SRA/McGraw-Hill. Permission is granted to reproduce this page for classroom use.